Fifty Golden Years

Fifty Golden Years
with my Yorkshire mistress

ASHLEY JACKSON

Dalesman

First published in 2006 by Dalesman
an imprint of
Country Publications Ltd
The Water Mill
Broughton Hall
Skipton
North Yorkshire
BD23 3AG

ISBN 1 85568 237 0

Repro by PPS Grasmere, Leeds
Printed by Compass Press, China

Picture credits:
Daily Mirror, page 9; Denis Thorpe, *Daily Mail*, page 10

Acknowledgements
The Ashley Jackson Gallery would like to thank all its clients over the
years for permission to reproduce the paintings in this book

Dedication
To life, and to Yorkshire for making me what I am

Contents

Preface

To Dad or AJ, both the same man:

I don't know why Dad asked me to write about him as he knows I am 'one of little words'. I have always been of the impression, why use five words when one will do? Although I have Dad's ability to verbalise and communicate, I didn't inherit his ability to be profound in prose.

Throughout my childhood I have been extremely fortunate. I have had conversations with L S Lowry, sung with Tony Christie and met John Major when he stopped off en route from Old Trafford to use our phone. My eyes have been opened to many countries and unforgettable experiences. But, when people have asked me 'What it is like living with Ashley Jackson?', I would say 'Dad's Dad'. The guy you meet at exhibitions, demonstrations or going to the post office in Holmfirth is the same man who raised my sister Heather and me. There is no difference. He may be philosophical and outspoken, but the most important thing that keeps him 'grounded' is family.

He will always say that the biggest achievement of his life is his family, his wife Anne, daughters and grandchildren, and there has been no moment in my life when I have ever doubted it.

Through his own traumatic childhood, he set out to sculpt the close family structure we share.

His passion and emotion are evident in his paintings, or 'love letters' as he prefers to call them. I could not be any prouder of my dad than I am, and the greatest accolade to his work would be that, long after the bloodline diminishes, on an overcast day with the sky about to storm, but with light streaming down through the darkness, people will look and say, 'That's an Ashley Jackson sky'.

Do we not all strive for immortality? Maybe Dad has found a way …

Claudia Jackson Berettoni

Foreword

ALL GOOD STORIES have a love affair somewhere within their pages. Bestsellers have a love story within a love story, and Ashley's love affair is not purely with his art but also with that most fickle, transient and demanding of mistresses — the unique beauty called Yorkshire.

If you are looking for the music-hall, archetypical Yorkshireman, you must look elsewhere. Ashley Jackson is no cloth-cap, wellies and ferret man. His passionate love for his home county is made manifest in his inquisitive need to delve into the secret heart of what is truly and uniquely the beauty of Yorkshire. Why would anyone sacrifice precious time, be frozen half to death and take an inordinate amount of care to depict what, to the rest of us, is just a cold, bleak moor-side, a few sparse trees and a derelict dwelling? A description sounds uninviting — until the addition of the Ashley factor. To spend time with Ashley's work is to experience his passion and insight as he captures that transient and dramatic beauty which is peculiar to Yorkshire and appeals to the true lover of this great county, both indigenous and adopted.

Ashley has been a member of the Yorkshire Society for many years, and has used his expertise, undoubted influence and his love of Yorkshire to assist the society to deliver its aims and objectives. To celebrate the society's silver jubilee, Ashley painted the famous Cow and Calf Rocks above Ilkley which has provided much-needed funds for promotional work. His appointment as a vice-president of the society has been well and truly earned, and he has set an example for future candidates.

Thank you, Ashley, for all you do for the county and for fifty years of capturing Yorkshire in all her glory — may there be many more to come.

Keith Madeley
Chairman, Yorkshire Society

Introduction

I WAS NINE years old when I first fell in love with the Yorkshire moors. My step-grandfather and grandmother's house was in Linthwaite, or what is called the Heights, in the Colne Valley. When I went to the back of the terrace houses and looked across the deep valley, and saw the trains like a miniature railway set, I thought 'Wow! If only I could paint that'. That was when I decided I wanted to be an artist. I can still visualise that view to this day.

At Holyrood Secondary School in Barnsley, South Yorkshire, my form teacher Miss Young took me in hand, and so did the art teacher Miss Netherwood, and I progressed under their guidance. In December 1955 I left Holyrood, and the headmaster Oswald Livesey and Miss Netherwood put me forward for Barnsley School of Art. I showed my portfolio to the art school head Harry Glover who, after taking one look at my work, offered me a place — without me even having to take the entrance exam.

There I was, aged seventeen, at art school. I knew that I couldn't finish the course without any money coming in, so I went to Ron Darwent, a local signwriter, and pestered him for a job. I must have been to see him about half a dozen times, and every time he would say 'I don't want anybody, I'm all right on my own'. Finally he said 'I'm bloody fed up with you — you start on Monday'.

That was my biggest break in the art world because it taught me discipline. Every dinnertime I used to go and practise my technique in the workshop: letter Os in one brush-stroke, for example, keeping the same thickness all the way round; getting all the verticals in every letter the same width; or writing backwards way round and inside out, because that's how we worked when lettering on solicitors' and accountants' windows.

Because there is no way to 'key' the paint on glass like there is with other mediums, you've got to control the brush with the liquid in and you've got to hold the brush to know how much you've got in there, or else it will run down the glass. Now, to paint a watercolour is simpler, because the paper gives you a 'key' to feel the brush dragging. Those early days gave me great experience in painting in watercolours, which I have always done vertically like I would letter on glass. Nobody else paints watercolours like that, but they may do now since they have seen me doing it on TV.

I hankered on about leaving Ron and becoming a proper artist in my own right. When I say 'proper artist', I was an artist

Above and left, Ashley in his studio at Dodworth, 1965.

with Ron, but I really wanted to be a watercolourist. So eventually I gave him six months' notice, thanked him for what he had done for me, and opened my own studio in Dodworth, near Barnsley. But Ron and I remained friends and have been for the past forty-odd years.

The studio work gradually took off, first with miners' banners — those were the days when the miners' galas were the big event of the year — or coffin plates and coffin vases in memory of some local person. I also painted people's pets, but I was never keen on the Yorkshire terriers because they used to

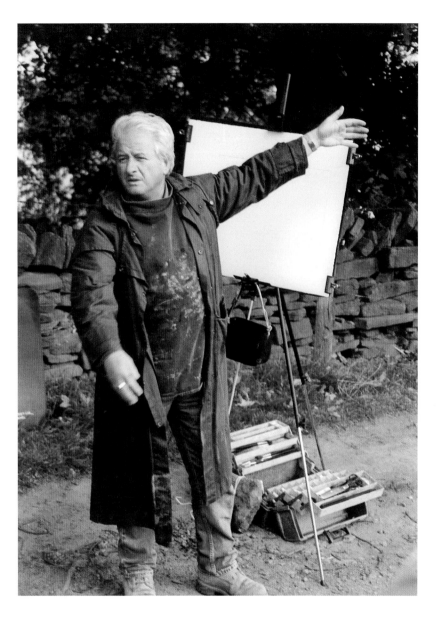

pee all over the studio. I did every piece of work that came my way, because I didn't know where my next bob was coming from.

I married my beloved Anne in 1962 and in 1968 we moved into a house at Silkstone Common. We vowed that we wouldn't

Facing page, painting at Top Withens, January 1972; above left, in Spain for Barry Cockcroft's 1979 YTV programme My Own Flesh and Blood; above, filming A Day Out with Ashley.

Ashley and daughter Claudia.

have any children until we got a bathroom. So for seven years we did not have any children. Heather was our first, naming her after the heather on the moors. (If she had been a boy, I would have called him Bracken.) Our second daughter, Claudia, was named after my grandmother who was a pianist.

At the same time I was hawking my works around London, driving down in a secondhand Post Office van in which I also slept, sleeping in Hyde Park in the van, going to Paddington Station for a wash and brush up. I did that for many, many years. Then one day in 1969 I went into the Upper Grosvenor Gallery in Park Lane. They were just hanging work by Dame Laura Knight, and it was the first time I had ever met anyone in a velvet suit. His name was Rodney Brangwyn and he was the great-nephew of Frank Brangwyn, the artist. He looked at my work and, to cut a long story short, within six weeks I would be having a one-man exhibition in Mayfair.

But the gallery wanted £2,500 key money for the catalogue, the staff, the champagne reception and so on —and the exhibition was only for one week. So I went to the Yorkshire Penny Bank, who had given us our mortgage, and asked to borrow the money. It meant that if the exhibition failed, we would have no house to live in, with one child and another on the way. Thankfully the exhibition was a success and the rest, as they say, is history.

We did that seven more times with the house — so eight times in total we risked our home on one game of pitch-and-toss, in effect. The last time was around fifteen years ago to finance the production of my TV series *A Brush with Ashley* for

Ashley at home.

Yorkshire Television. My first appearance on television, though, was back in 1968 on *Omnibus*. I have also been on *Pebble Mill at One* for a forty-eight week run — all going out live — but the best TV programme I was ever involved with was Barry Cockcroft's documentary *Once in a Lifetime – My Own Flesh and Blood*. We went in search of my roots, first in the Dales, then in Spain and Ireland. From there I worked for many years with Yorkshire Television on *A Brush with Ashley*.

Throughout my career I have tried to be the people's artist. I want my paintings to be accessible. They don't need to have a dictionary by their side explaining why I've done them. I keep out of the art establishments. I don't want to be a herd animal. I want to be free as a bird. And to be able to say what I want and think what I want, and to paint what I want.

It is the Yorkshire people, and people who love Yorkshire, who have always given me that support, and that is why I am here today, still painting. So I owe everything to the county of Yorkshire — and my mistress the Yorkshire moors in particular — for the last fifty golden years.

Ashley Jackson
Holmfirth, 2006

Early spring, Dentdale

THE MEADOWS DOTTED with their flocks of sheep as lambing time approaches gives you the feeling of a fresh start to life.

It always takes me back to a young man and his new wife, camping in Muker, Swaledale. We were sitting in the Farmers Arms, with the fire roaring up the chimney and a good pint of Yorkshire ale pulled by the landlord, Donald France. He was a larger-than-life character, an old English gentleman who had served in the forces in India and had that old colonial feeling.

In came a parson and his young wife. He had never ventured into Yorkshire in his life before. He ordered half a beer and, turning to Donald, asked 'Are you the landlord?' He emptied his pockets and put the contents on the table alongside my beer and sandwiches, saying 'What are these, landlord? We have found many in the fields we have been walking through.'

Donald turned to me and said, with a glint in his eye, 'Are you going to tell him or am I?'

I explained to the young parson, delicately as I could coming from Barnsley, that these so-called 'rubber bands', which were all over our table, were for castrating the rams.

As I looked at him, whilst telling him this, he shyly emptied all his pockets of these rubber bands, like a young boy emptying string, conkers and old sweets out of his pocket — to much merriment in the pub.

So this painting of spring in Dentdale will be my memorial to Donald France, with whom Anne and I had many a memorable meeting over pints of ale.

The railway viaduct and River Dee near Stonehouse, Dentdale

THE DEE WHICH flows through Dentdale is a lovely, winding, meandering river, where you can see children turning over stones looking for hidden fish, as you would in Enid Blyton's 'Famous Five' stories, or racing twigs as speedboats over the white surf to a finishing point — a gentle river.

I chose this composition because it depicts man with nature: the railway which meanders through the dale, over viaducts and through tunnels, in competition with the River Dee. As the river moves patiently through the valley, we should learn from Mother Nature about hurrying here and hurrying there, with no time to stop and stare.

STONEHOUSE, DENTDALE 17

Featherbed Moss, Langsett Moor

AS A YOUNG boy of fourteen, I trod these moors over from Margery Hill to Cutgate. I always wanted to depict their vastness. Some people would call it emptiness because of the lack of trees and buildings, but I have always felt treading on the spongy, soaked moor very spiritual, giving the feeling one is very close to the maker.

West Nab and Deer Hill from Wessenden Head Moor

I HAVE ALWAYS been fascinated and enthralled with painting and reading skies, as I feel that a sky changes within seconds. To be able to capture the shape and movements, you have to absorb the spirit and atmosphere. I feel you can only achieve this by reading Mother Nature's love letters. Ever since I trod the moors, I have been fortunate to be able to sense this feeling.

We as civilised human beings find all our senses eroding — the sense of touch, smell, sound, sight. Putting these all together, I feel, makes you aware of your inner self.

I have often said that, when I paint the moors, the hairs on the back of my hand have to stand rigidly. If they don't, I have created a picture rather than a painting, and immediately tear it up.

The beauty here is of West Nab and Deer Hill. In the background, Castle Hill (Huddersfield's most famous landmark) stands out majestically and can be seen for miles around. The day had a windswept, typical West Riding atmosphere. The only company I had was a curlew in flight.

The painting should speak a thousand words.

The Druid Stone near the Lion Inn, Blakey Ridge

I VIVIDLY REMEMBER coming upon this stone while taking part in the Lyke Wake Walk from Osmotherley to Ravenscar. I had left Barnsley with my old boss Ron Darwent. He was an outdoor fiend who introduced me to the Dales and North York Moors during camping expeditions.

It was cold and bleak when we set off in late evening, having travelled up from Barnsley after finishing work to complete the walk within twenty-four hours to become a 'dirger'. It was the same weekend that the well-loved President, John F Kennedy, was assassinated in Dallas on the 23rd November 1963. As we drove to Osmotherley we were stunned to hear the news of the President's shooting. When we met up with the rest of the party who were accompanying us on the walk, we all seemed to agree that it felt like we were on the verge of World War Three.

As we walked through the darkness of the night, picking our way across the moor with our torches and compasses, we felt like true explorers — a far different experience to the Lyke Wake Walk today, which has a well-signed and -trodden path.

Over the horizon we saw dark figures dancing to a lantern theatre. We joked and wondered if they were moon men coming towards us. They were actually five SAS commandos in full kit. We stopped and asked about the state of Kennedy, and were told he had passed away, which in the days of the Cold War made us feel even more cold and unprotected walking on the roof of Yorkshire.

Walking the moor at night with the wind howling does give you great inspiration and the power to paint. That is what I have always searched for — the drama of the moor.

I had to paint the Druid Stone in the cold of the winter, the snow revealing human life that once trod this path and left its mark on the unforgiving landscape. It was a cold and frosty morning; snow had fallen overnight and the clouds were clearing, giving a wilderness of blue and white light coming from the heavens. There was a stillness as sharp as the frost on the moor. When my movements to set up my easel startled a grouse into screaming out like a human being, I thought I had awakened the giant with his stone finger penetrating the sky.

The Druid Stone stands as a mark of remembrance to all who pass this place for time immemorial, like a finger penetrating through the soil and snow warning us selfish human beings that, if we do not heed Mother Nature's warnings, we will have no moor to walk on.

Brown light on Langsett Moor

I TRIED TO capture the brown, polluted clouds caused by industry which gives a warmth of colour without the sun.

Capturing the three to four depths of cloud from foreground, middle distance, distance and infinity, the sky and clouds to me are heavenly landscapes, now polluted by man.

Twenty-five years ago Barry Cockcroft, the author and documentary film-maker, and personal friend of mine, wrote:

'Never in his outstanding career as a professional painter, which spans a quarter of a century, has Ashley wrapped himself and his art in an aloof, protective mantle like so many of his contemporaries: he does not infer, and never has, that artistic talent is handed down to certain individuals by the gods and can never be truly acquired by ordinary mortals.'

Barden Tower, Wharfedale

WHAT DREW ME to paint this scene, which always reminds me of our Yorkshire heritage, were the towers catching what spare light there was, picking out the sheep in the field and the wall toppings leading towards Barden Tower. The gnarled tree on the left-hand-side foreground tells the story of what harsh winters we have.

The trees in the middle distance are also picked out by the light, which gives them an edge to the ones in the background, the rain clouds moving away to invite the warm sky.

Raining, Langsett Moor

LANGSETT MOOR ALWAYS takes me back to my youth. We used to go for long hikes over to the Derwent Valley and back, then catch the bus home to Barnsley. So I can say it is one of my most memorable and favourite moors.

In the painting you can see, through the cold, dank, misty rain, the far horizon. Your heart would sink into your sodden boots at the thought of having to reach that distant goal before gaining the luxury of a seat on the bus to take you home.

That's why, in this Langsett Moor painting, I have a 'silver lining' in the windswept clouds — the painting says it all.

Summer's day, the George Inn, Hubberholme

A TYPICAL YORKSHIRE holiday where the sky would break and through this window in the sky would come shafts of sunlight — only to disappear again. Then the moorland grit would fall from the sky and make you sodden in your boots.

This was the day I planned to capture the George in bright sunlight, but it was not to be.

On Greenfield Moor with West Nab

YOU WILL HAVE noted from my paintings that I love huge skies: the skies you get, I feel, only on the Yorkshire moors (the Pennine backbone of England). They have fascinated me from being a boy of nine years old.

In this particular painting, I have tried to capture the window of light shaping the heavenly sky with that band of light in the distance silhouetting West Nab, which a photographer would call backlighting.

The light falling onto the moor gives a warmth to the bracken which bends to the wind.

Down from Cutgate Moor

You may wonder, then ask the question: Why do you paint the drama of the soft light time and time again? My answer would be: Because I love what I call soft light into diffused light and I am forever chasing it through my life in painting.

As a young man, I wrote these words in 1956:

'I have always said, right from sixteen years of age, that I would never want to be the "Genius of the Chocolate Box", never want to paint pictures but paintings, as paintings have the soul of the artist in them. Pictures are mechanically constructed.'

The approaching storm, Swaledale Moor

MOORLAND WALLS HAVE always fascinated me, as they weave a pattern over the moor and outline the contours.

I not only find them helpful in a painting, but also in sheltering me from storms. I use them as a windbreak against the elements and fight for a position with the sheep sometimes edging me out to get a warm place.

To capture this dark, moorland sky rolling towards me, my makeshift shelter came in very handy.

Misty light, Cutgate

THIS IS WHERE you come to the edge of the moor, which I call Surprise View because you see the Derwent Valley and all the moorland fells looking like islands in the mist.

'The sun will burn you,
The rain will wet you,
The wind will chill you,
But only people make you cry.
So paint what you feel and not
What will sell.'

Ashley Jackson, 1962

Dark clouds over Cam Houses

CAM HOUSES REMINDS me of the day when I left my young wife Anne in our static caravan, owned by the warm-hearted Mrs Hesseldine, at Henry's, the Green, Hawes.

It was a beautiful sunny morning as I drove out of the gates in my red MGB Drophead, making my way to Cam. On reaching the Roman road, I parked the car and continued on foot to this remote hamlet, excited by the prospect of painting on a fine summer morning.

I didn't realise what a sensitive person I was until I started to sketch the old hamlet, feeling as though I was not on my own but with people from the past looking on, and children playing in the fields around. All of a sudden the skies blackened. It was as though someone had switched off the light — I was in a coal cellar, feeling the darkness and smelling the mustiness.

Running for shelter from the storm to an old barn, speaking out loud to myself I said, 'I must get out of here as quickly as possible'. I had a feeling which I have never been able to explain. Running up the fell to my awaiting escape jalopy with the lightning striking the moor all around, getting to my MGB which had its roof off, squelching in my seat, having no time to put the roof up, I drove like a maniac back down to Hawes where, believe it or not, the sun was still shining.

The experience I had made me feel unwelcome to do any paintings of Cam Houses that day.

Roman road, Wheeldale Moor

THE ROMAN ROAD is part of the Lyke Wake Walk which I completed in the weekend President John F Kennedy was assassinated. Each painting tells a story words cannot express.

'When a man does a piece of work which is admired by all, we say that it is wonderful; but when we see the changes of day and night, the sun, the moon, and the stars in the sky, and the changing seasons upon the earth, with their ripening fruits, anyone must realise that it is the work of someone more powerful than Man.'

Chased-by-Bears (1843-1915), Santee-Yanktonai Sioux

ROMAN ROAD, WHEELDALE MOOR 43

Middlesmoor, Nidderdale

NIDDERDALE I AM fond of as it's a little gem of a dale. I remember as a young man learning to drive, motoring up to Howe Stean Gorge on business with my old boss, Ron Darwent, in a little Mini van. I was due to take my driving test the next day. I passed, and feel I owed it all to that drive from Barnsley up and down to Nidderdale.

For a base we used the Yorke Arms, where Yorkshire fayre is in abundance, more so the hospitality. Situated where it is, the inn is an ideal base from which to trek; whichever direction you choose, there is a painting to be painted.

In this painting of Middlesmoor I have tried to capture the warmth of light hitting the distance and foreground with its contrasting dark shadows cast from the skies above. The sheep in the meadow face the warm glow of the sun.

MIDDLESMOOR, NIDDERDALE 45

Storm over Garsdale

I PLACE MYSELF among the luckiest people on God's earth, to be able to stand on a windswept moor looking at the scene I am about to paint with all its glory and reverence. I have often said I paint in the great cathedral of the open air, and when you see such a scene as this on Garsdale Moor I do believe there is a controlling force.

Snowstorm, the Lion Inn, North Yorkshire

I FIRST CAUGHT sight of the Lion Inn when doing the Lyke Wake Walk one November night when the rain was sweeping across the moor. It was from this walk across the North York Moors that I got the inspiration for my paintings.

'This yah neet, this yah neet,
Ivvery neet an' all,
Fire an' fleet an' cannle leet,
An' Christ tak up thy saul.

Fra Whinny Moor when thoo art passed,
Ivvery neet an' all,
Ti t' Brig o' Dreead thoo cums at last,
An' Christ tak up thy soul.'

Richard Blakeborough's version of the 'Cleveland Lyke Wake Dirge'.
The funny thing is that the Lion Inn is nicknamed Blakey.

Down from Wessenden

WALKING DOWN FROM Wessenden Head is a path which takes you to Marsden. It is through a beautiful valley that ordinary country lovers know — one I call my secret valley.

I have tried to depict and capture with a very limited palette the tonal value which gives me the shape of the landscape and what's in it.

The light on this day was quite diffused and coming from all angles, playing tricks and games with my eyes. This I always feel is a challenge — as we say in Yorkshire, 'dasty'. The challenge was mine to take up and enjoy. This is the beauty of painting in the outdoors, for every day is a challenge to put your wit and soul in harmony — to express in painting what you are trying to say.

Upper Midhope, Langsett

WE WERE JUST coming back from a long walk over the moor, Heather, my eldest daughter, and I, up this shady green lane — a little gem of a hideaway. You can always find these little jewels in the landscape if you use your eyes for seeing and not just looking. I have said countless times that many people look but only a few see.

Spring was just around the corner, the sunlight was illuminating the patches of vivid green moss and grass like a stage set, and the trees reminded me of the *Wind in the Willows*. I couldn't help but stop and capture the moment.

On the moor, Wharfedale

THE WIND WAS swirling round me as though Mother Nature did not want me to depict the landscape I saw in front of me. High above Wharfedale, away from the madding crowd, to feel what the spirit of the moor was trying to say to me was quite eerie. The painting should say it all.

ON THE MOOR, WHARFEDALE   55

Ponden, near Haworth

THE NAME HAWORTH has always conjured up in my mind the image of Wuthering Heights, but Ponden is only a few miles from Top Withens. It snugly nestles between the valleys with its tall trees protected by the hills which, like the walls around the Secret Garden, offer protection from the winds to the surrounding vegetation and people who dwell there.

I have tried to capture the limited light on a summer's evening, but incidentally warm light coming from the left-hand side of the painting like a torch lights up the browns and the greens.

Evening light, Langsett Moor to Cutgate

'Dreaming when Dawn's left hand was in the sky
I heard a voice within the tavern cry
"Awake, my little ones, and fill the cup
Before Life's liquor in its cup be dry".'

Omar Khayyam

EVENING LIGHT, LANGSETT MOOR TO CUTGATE 59

Low light, before the storm, Featherbed Moss

'Time is for ever —
There is no death, only
a change of place:
to see and feel the moor
to see light and feel and
smell the bracken
let alone paint it
is indeed an honour.'

Ashley Jackson

The browns and reds of the moor — above the Holme Valley

IT IS AMAZING what the play of light can do. Whatever colour the sky or the landscape has in it, it is reflected from one to the other. I always love to paint in reflected light, where the light bounces down from the sky and tints the moor.

Warm rain — Black Hill, Holme Moss

ON THE MOORS of Yorkshire, quite often you will get a wisp of light on the horizon, which I call a saucepan lid sky — it's as if a saucepan lid has been lifted half an inch from the earth to expose a sharp light from within.

In this painting I experienced something a little different. The moor is on the horizon with mist forming in the valley between it and myself. It seemed like the distant moor was an island in the mist.

Greenfield Moor

THERE IS SUNSHINE in the dark shadows ... and to me that is
what life is all about.

If you walk only on sunny days you will never reach your
destination.

Storm on its way, Pennine Way

THIS TRACK LEADS over to Marsden from Black Hill. I have tried to capture the wind sweeping across the sky, pulling the clouds and feathering them as a watercolour artist would do.

Only by seeing, can Mother Nature help you in forming your painting. There is no way one can set up an easel without it being blown away.

Farms in Garsdale

'Yorkshire, if not for you
I would not be an artist.
You are the one who made my eyes see and my heart feel.
Friends will leave, but you will stay long after my days have gone.
So glad I am to see you without my chair or my table,
through my six-inch-square window then only to see the 'Wall'.
But your soul creeps in through the bars, the TV cameras, the guards
and it's your soul and only yours that keeps me sane!
If I lost my eyes I would keep you in my soul.'

Ashley Jackson, 1st July 1971

'When all have left me
I will still have you, my Yorkshire.'

12th December 1970

'If you are sensitive you will be an artist,
If you are not then you will be a painter.'

17th November 1971

Wainstalls, near Halifax

WHILE STANDING ON Wainstall Moor looking across to Stood-ley Pike, feeling more and more passionate about my mistress — Yorkshire — I was fortunate to see her in her glory with a multitude of indigos and light blues falling from the sky and marrying into the distant landscape of the high Pennines.

This is indeed a feeling that no material possession can ever thrill you with. It touches your inner soul.

Long shadows — the George Inn, Hubberholme

I HAVE ALWAYS had a soft spot for the George Inn nestling in Hubberholme, with the trees around it and the shoulders of the fells like some God-fearing mammal protecting it from the elements. I have spent some happy hours over the years at the inn with my wife Anne and my family.

Paths over to Garsdale Moor in the direction of Hawes

IT WAS A rainy, misty morning when I tried to capture this scene, where the mist slowly shrouds the moor, playing tricks — now you see it, now you don't. The sheep are quietly grazing unperturbed by what Mother Nature throws at them. I happened to catch sight of a curlew in the mist, which just made the painting.

Nature's art, Greenfield Moor

WE MERE HUMAN beings cannot perfect or compete with nature's artistic ability. She can make beautiful shapes in sculpture out of the powdered snow, leaving the moor like frozen seas.

I captured this window of light reflecting down onto the frozen landscape where two sheep were digging for food.

The Cottage, Hardcastle Crags

THE COTTAGE NESTLING just on the edge of the wooded valley
is a lovely hideaway from the township of Hebden Bridge, and
only a few miles from Top Withens.

I always thought, as a young boy, I would end my life living in
an idyllic situation like this. I have tried to capture the peaceful-
ness of this isolated cottage.

High Withens: Wuthering Heights

STANLEY CHAPMAN WAS the one who took Anne and me up to High Withens in 1966.

I feel that, every time I try to paint this Yorkshire scene, much as I try the thing never comes out right. I try to put atmosphere in my paintings (atmosphere that only Yorkshire has) but as much as I endeavour, I feel I lose it. I don't want to become 'The Genius of the Chocolate Box'. I go mad every time a painting is completed.

I have never been satisfied with any of my work, Lord knows why people want to buy it. Painting has become a drug to me and like a drug it has side-effects that not everyone sees but my wife Anne.

'The heights by great men reached and kept
Were not attained by sudden flight,
But they, while their companions slept,
Were toiling upward in the night.'

Henry Wadsworth Longfellow

The Cow and Calf on Ilkley Moor

TO EVERY YORKSHIRE person, this piece of landscape will be sacred to them. The very place made famous by the Yorkshire anthem 'On Ilkley Moor Baht 'At'.

I was honoured and privileged to paint this scene for the twenty-fifth anniversary of the Yorkshire Society. I wanted to capture the wind in my hair and the sweet smell of the moor.

Scammonden Moor

I COULD NOT help but remember my days as a youthful artist, walking these moors, getting lost in its loveable landscape.

On looking back with sentimental feeling for the day, I was commissioned by Ivan Hirst, who worked for the British embassy in Paris. This was his family home, which was due to be demolished to make way for Scammonden Dam.

Showing what a small world it is, Barbara Castle's ministerial advisor, who was with her at the British embassy in Paris, said: 'Isn't that an Ashley Jackson painting?' On hearing this, it went to my head like a pint of Barnsley bitter.

Spurn Point, at the mouth of the Humber

WHERE THE North Sea meets the River Humber. I wanted to capture this magnificent lighthouse as a beacon to humanity, fighting to survive all that the elements throw at it. Unfortunately there will come a day when this peninsula is once again an island, or disappears. So I had to capture it.

Boggle Hole, North Yorkshire coast

A GOOD FRIEND of mine, Ron Darwent, would go with me on long country walks, and I would take my paints and pencils. We laughed at Boggle Hole, because for the sake of our art we nearly died. I was doing a watercolour sketch from the rocks and did not notice that the tide was slowly (like a snake) creeping in behind Ron and I. We only realised within seconds of having to swim to shore, with our climbing boots and rucksacks. Those are my very vivid memories of Boggle Hole.

Flight Hill, above Holmfirth

I FEEL THAT the farm on Flight Hill clings to the moor and faces
up to whatever nature throws at it: the wind, the rain, the snow.
This to me builds the character of the folk who scratch their
living up in, what I call, the swell of the moor. As I have always
said, Yorkshire's Pennines are like frozen seas, and I feel the
farm on Flight Hill is like a fishing boat working with Mother
Nature to survive.

FLIGHT HILL, ABOVE HOLMFIRTH   93

Storm, snow and light, Saddleworth Moor

YOU CAN SEE the cathedral window of light which helped me compose the painting, with the moorland wall in the foreground buried shoulder-deep with just the dark line of the wall toppings showing. It weaves past the two sheep into the horizon where the light from the window catches the distant moor, giving me the depth I was looking for.

Upper Wharfedale, near Grassington

THE VIEW OF the River Wharfe just north of Grassington winding itself through the dale named after it, with the woodlands in the valley, stretching as far as the eye can see.

This was a commission I did for the Woodland Trust.

Up from Marsden

A LOVELY FARMSTEAD on the outskirts of Marsden. I tried to capture the evening in November (well, it was late afternoon, as we have short days at that time of year). I was attracted to the silhouette of the gable end of the farm, but most of all the trees laced in the sky.

Looking at winter trees on the uplands of Yorkshire reminds me of those lives which have gone by — of hands and fingers penetrating the earth, and reaching out to the heavens.

Watercolour memories of Yorkshire: Wolfstones, Holme Valley

THIS BEAUTIFUL FARMSTEAD lies a couple of miles from where we live. In watercolour, one looks at light and shade to give you shape. It was a grey winter's afternoon and Mother Nature helped me immensely. The dark and light tones disappeared away from me. I didn't have to do any work at all in translating what stood before me.

Mother Nature made it simple for me to capture this day.

Hade Edge near Holmfirth with Castle Hill in the distance

I KNOW THAT the Romans came here long before me, but they have left their mark on many a moorland road — straight as a die, giving the illusion it is flat, whereas in some cases it is really a helter skelter.

I always revert back to my old friend and mentor L S Lowry when discussing optical illusions. He said: 'When you are painting it, if you do it right, and it looks wrong in your painting, then it is wrong. If, however, you do it wrong, but it looks right in the painting, then it's right … What's the fuss?'.

You can see Castle Hill in the distance, with the last of the surviving mill chimneys in the valley, a monumental memorial to the hard life which has passed us by.

I love drystone walls that snake into the distance. I have tried to capture the winter shadows of the clouds dancing on the roads.

Town Head, near Dunford Bridge

TOWN HEAD ONCE housed the navvies who built the railways.
The Dunford tunnels lie at the bottom of the hill. The tunnels
fused Yorkshire and Lancashire together. You have to admire
the skill and quality of the Victorians who built and engineered
what we may call works of art. But we must remember there
were many people killed and maimed while completing them.
So my painting of Town Head is a homage to those navvies and
engineers.

When God moves — storm over Deer Hill

HERE YOU WILL see the controlling force of a power far greater than us, which makes me feel very humble to be in the audience of great theatrical movements.

I have tried to capture the light from the heavens caressing the moorland and reflecting back to contrast with the dark, forbidding sky. I feel as though I am in a kaleidoscope of dark and light tones. I feel quite insignificant when trying to capture in watercolour what I experienced and felt.

Littlecake Lane, near Boshaw, Holmfirth

I HAD ALWAYS wanted to paint this wooded part of the moor. What drew me to it, more than just the moorland and its position on the moor, was the name of the lane. It sounds as though it comes from the child's storybook *The Wind in the Willows*, with its summer sky, fluffy clouds sailing by like galleons, the breeze making the trees dance against the moorland horizon, taking me back to my childhood of long, hot, carefree summer days.

Winter, West Nab

HIGH ABOVE HOLMFIRTH is a lovely stretch of moor called Wessenden. From here you will see nature play with light in such a way that for an artist it really makes you feel that there is a controlling force.

One minute you will see the distant hill fade away into the mist, the next it reappears. It is this sort of atmosphere that I have tried to capture. As I have said before: read Mother Nature's love letters which she is trying to write to all of us. I hope that you may be able to read through my painting what she is trying to tell us.

Summer — Ponden Reservoir, near Haworth

I WANTED TO capture the late summer's day with the warm light, hitting the cottages and the tops of the trees, beginning to fade. I wanted to give the feeling of tranquillity, where no motor cars shatter the peace of the moment, as if the Brontës were still going about their business.

Snowstorm on the moors, *Flight Hill*

FOR MANY YEARS I have enjoyed the changing skies over Flight Hill, which lies above Winscar Reservoir, a few miles from Holmfirth.

I have tried to capture the skies with all the drama and strength that prevails. The more I stand and paint in the high pastures of moorland Yorkshire, the more I feel the spirit of the moor.

Only when I feel her and sense her do I try and execute a painting. I know when this happens physically because the hairs on the back of my arms stand up rigid as when you hear a piece of music that enthrals you. I try very much to capture the heart and soul of my beloved moor.

In this painting, you will see that the movement of the sky is so strong and powerful that it gives you mere moments to see and capture the window of light which plays a great part in creating shape and movement. If there is no light, there is no depth.

Rain on the way, Cam Houses

ONE WONDERS WHY this moorland hamlet, looking down towards Wharfedale, seems to draw me back time and time again over the years. I must admit I do have an affection for this little place which has weathered the storms and all that Mother Nature has thrown at it. Painting here I can still hear the children playing on the open moorland, drowning out the sounds of mother calling them in to tea.

On the road to Burnsall, Wharfedale, near Barden Hall

IT WAS A warm autumn afternoon when I captured the scene of
stillness in the air — wispy cloud and birds in flight, the sky
squeezing the last precious autumn light before winter's arrival.

When the wind blows — Cutgate, Langsett Moor

I HAVE KNOWN this moor from boyhood, when my pals and I would hike over Margery Hill onto Cutgate and down into the big valley of the Derwent, where we'd have our sandwiches with a bottle of pop then take off our clothes and go for a swim, even on a misty day. Keeping our eye out for the moorland wardens, we'd dry ourselves off with the wind and the sun — we never thought to take towels. We'd then walk over the moor with the dusk turning to darkness, seeing the Flouch Inn, which we were making for, pointed out to us by vehicle head-lights, shining like glow-worms on the horizon. Then from the Flouch, we'd catch a bus to Barnsley and home.

Now I know those days as rocking-chair memories.

Crossley Moor, West Nab in the distance

'Talking to a great friend of mine, Jack Brown, today about life and art, we feel and have the same feelings about it. You must be sincere in what you do. I get a lot of inspiration from him. I know confidence is something I have not got, and Jack tries to put it in me. I am a cap-in-hand man.'

4th February 1968

'It gets wild on the moor' — Saddleworth Moor

One of the most difficult things I have tried to capture is the tunnel of light Mother Nature plays tricks with, wanting you to see what she wants you to see.

It takes me back to the days the lovely gentleman James R Gregson (Dick Gregson to his pals), the Yorkshire playwright from Brighouse, said that I painted 'echoes' in my work, which is just as essential to a writer as to an artist to keep the interest going.

I find it is very easy to paint something such as a tree, a barn, a wall in fields, but very difficult to paint nothing — the flat Yorkshire moor with no man-made feature in it. Less is more. You will see in this book my experiences of the misty moor with the soft moving light portraying to me a more spiritual being. I can understand the Brontë sisters being so enthralled with it to want to put to pen to paper, for I have tried for half a century to depict it in watercolour.

The storm in the snow, Saddleworth Moor

AS A YOUNG man I always believed in trying to capture the soul, rather than pretty pictures. Pictures, as you will know, are mechanically constructed. A painting should try to capture the soul of the landscape from the soul of the artist.

I feel so sorry for the sheep on these moors, digging for food to survive. How can they exist in conditions like this, that make me dig deep into my pocket for my beloved flask of whisky? — purely for medicinal purposes of course. However, the whisky is added to my water pot so when I paint in cold weather the watercolours do not freeze. I could add meths but I am not a meths drinker.

THE STORM IN THE SNOW, SADDLEWORTH MOOR   127

Mist on the moor, Greenfield Moor

I FELL IN love with the swirling mist, giving me echoes of light, feeling as though I was looking through various tunnels, and getting a great pleasure of seeing Mother Nature in moods I am only privileged to see. I feel so sad that many human beings have to pay to be entertained. Here in the great cathedral of the open air, in the theatre of light, you see things money just can't buy.

The tracks of the Pennine Way play with your eyesight: you see them crisp and clear in the foreground, then in a moment they disappear and you see the horizon crisp and clear. I have said often that many people look, but few see. This gift, if only we knew, is for all of us to enjoy who are born with the gift of sight.

Raining on Langsett Moor

There is not much I can say in words about the light on the moor combining with my feeling for the moor than repeat the lines I wrote on the 17th October, 1968:

'"Love who has us in his net, can we dream and not forget?"
(Tennyson)
for LIFE is dreams, which we will not forget.
When we who stand on the moor see dreams of bygone LIFE for sure.
For we see ourselves as ourselves, and not as people see us.
Love who has us in his net,
for we have loved and shall not forget.
Society and civilisations are Drugs which may be taken, but not to addiction, for remember we are man and woman who have instincts, feelings, and tears.
Love who has us in his net has given us dreams that we can't forget.
So to hell with society and be Human …
Feel the land for the land will feel all of us one day
For life is dreams which we will not regret.'

Window in the sky — deep blue light on Greenfield Moor

'My Love for the Moors of Yorkshire:
One must watch — what good is it if you gain the whole world and
lose your soul.
Yorkshire has really got a strong hold on me.
But why should I let her go, and where would I be if she was not there?
People can hurt you but the moors won't, yet the moors might kill you.
But if you know the moors and their moods, you will grow to love them
far deeper then anything.'

1970

'The only thing is that enthusiasm may be taken for big-
headedness by some small-minded people.'

1970

Exhibitions, TV programmes and publications

One-man exhibitions

1963	Brighouse
1964	Newark Art Gallery, Nottingham
1966	Crows Nest Gallery, Dewsbury
1967	Brighouse Art Gallery
1968	Wakefield Art Gallery
1968	Cannon Hall Gallery, Barnsley
1969	Upper Grosvenor Gallery, West End, London
1974	The Mall Gallery, FBA, London
1977	Municipal Gallery, Valencia, Spain
1978	Kidderminster Art Gallery
1979	Maclaurin Gallery, Glasgow, Scotland
1979	Foyles Gallery, Charing Cross Road, London
1983	The Old Barn, Ruislip
1984	Milan
1984	Washington, USA
1985	Dallas, USA
1985	New York, USA
1985	Chicago, USA
1986	Milan
1986	*Ashley Jackson's Vision of Turner*, Mall Gallery, FBA, West End, London. Sponsored by the *Yorkshire Post*.
1987	Cooper Art Gallery, Barnsley
1987	San Francisco, USA
1987	*Ashley Jackson's Vision of Turner*. Opened by HRH the Prince of Wales; sponsored by Bass.
1988	New York, USA
1989	St Louis, USA
1990	*My Way, Art to the People*, retrospective exhibition, Huddersfield Art Gallery. Sponsored by Yorkshire TV.
1991	*In Mood with the Moor*, Lauron Gallery, Ilkley
1991	*In Harmony with the Moor*, John Worthy Gallery, Leek
1992	The Coach House Gallery, Lincoln
1993	United Society of Artists, London
1993	Patchings Art Gallery, Nottingham
1994	Yorkshire Post HQ, Leeds
1994	*My Mistress and I — The Yorkshire Moors*, Rotherham Art Gallery
1995	*Here's to you, Dad*, Cooper Art Gallery, Barnsley; touring exhibition to Smith Gallery, Brighouse, Dewsbury Town Hall and Doncaster Art Gallery
1996	*From Yorkshire with Love*, Beningbrough Hall, York, Wakefield Art Gallery, Sewerby Hall, Bridlington
1997	*Earth, Wind and Fire*, Salford Art Gallery
1999	*Twilight of the Twentieth Century*, Cartwright Hall, Bradford
2000	*Dawns a New Day*, Royal Armouries, Leeds
2006	South Kirby Council, two-man show with Graham Ibbeson
2006	West End, London, two-man show with Graham Ibbeson, sponsored by Clydesdale Bank

Group shows/mixed exhibitions

Royal Watercolour Society, Open Exhibition, London

Royal Institute of Painters in Watercolour, Open Exhibition, London

Britain in Watercolour, Federation of British Artists, Open Exhibition — work was chosen for touring exhibition

Yorkshire Watercolour Society, Harrogate Art Gallery

House of Commons

Lowry Gallery, Salford, Manchester, Mixed

Below: Ashley and Anne (expecting their daughter Heather) at the opening of Ashley's gallery in Church Street, Barnsley, in 1968. Opposite: HRH the Prince of Wales, with Ashley and Anne, opening the 1987 exhibition Ashley Jackson's Visions of Turner in Yorkshire. (© Huddersfield Examiner.)

exhibition with sculptor Sam Tonkis

1974, guest exhibitor by invitation in exhibition at Lanzarote, Spain, featuring Picasso, Dali and Miro

United Society of Artists, London

1995 (and 1996), Beverley Minster Fine Art Exhibition

Television productions

1968   *Omnibus* programme, BBC

1978   (and 1985) own television series on *Pebble Mill at One*, BBC

1981   *Once in a Lifetime – My own Flesh and Blood*, documentary, ITV

1982   *Making the Most of …*

1984   (to 1988) *Ashley Jackson's World of Art*, three six-part series on Yorkshire TV

1990   *Profile of an Artist*, BBC Look North

1990   *A Brush with Ashley*, his own series on Yorkshire TV

1992   *A Brush with Ashley*, second series, Yorkshire TV and satellite

1993   *A Brush with Ashley*, third series

1990   (to 1996) *A Brush with Ashley*, the Learning Channel, satellite TV

1994   mini-series, Wire TV

1995   *A Brush with Ashley*, fourth series

1997   *A View with Ashley*, fifth series

1998   *A View with Ashley*, sixth series

1999   *A View with Ashley*, seventh series

2000   *A View with Ashley*, eighth series
        Ashley Jackson's Yorkshire, Yorkshire TV

Books published

1981   *My Brush with Fortune — an artist's notebook*, Secker and Warburg

1989   *Ashley Jackson's World of Art*, volumes 1, 2, and 3, Alexandra Art Corporation, USA.

1992   *Painting in the Open Air*, Harper Collins

1993   *A Brush with Ashley*, Box Tree Publications

1994   *Painting the British Isles — a Watercolourist's Journey*, Box Tree Publications

2000   *Ashley Jackson's Yorkshire Moors — a love affair*, Dalesman

2006   *Fifty Golden Years: with my Yorkshire mistress*, Dalesman

Entries

Who's Who in Art
Debretts' People of Today
Burke's

Honours

1996   Ashley was a former student of Barnsley School of Art, and in his honour they established the Ashley Jackson Gallery on their site at Barnsley College, housing twenty-six originals by Ashley. The gallery is open to the public on Friday evenings from 3.30-5pm.

1996   Yorkshire Awards for Art and Entertainment

2005   Freedom of the City of London

2005   Vice-president of the Yorkshire Society

Above: Ashley with Dame Norma Major at his sixtieth birthday exhibition Dawns a New Day at the Royal Armouries, Leeds, in 2000.

Opposite: Ashley with Lady and Sir Bernard Ingham at Salford Art Gallery in 1987. Sir Bernard officially opened Ashley's exhibition Earth, Wind and Fire.

Index